Oceans of Hope
Awakening the World to Marine Litter

Tania Winther

@atelierwinther

ISBN: 9798854710190

Imprint: Independently published

KDP Publishing

www.atelierwinther.no/poetry

All poetry and prose is written by the author. Illustrations are contributions by several artists including the author.
Credits are given to each of the artists who have contributed to this project.
* The illustration on the book cover is A.I.generated

Water, oh water, so clear and so blue,
Flowing and glistening, it's a wonder to view.
From mountains to oceans, it travels with grace,
A life-giving force, it sustains every race.
In streams and in rivers, it dances and swirls,
A symphony of motion, as it twists and twirls.
In falls and in rapids, it roars and it crashes,
A power so mighty, no one can surpass it.
In lakes and in ponds, it lies calm and serene,
A peaceful oasis, a sight to be seen.
In oceans and seas, it ebbs and it flows,
A force to be reckoned with, wherever it goes.
Water, oh water, so vital and true,
A giver of life, sustaining me and you.
So let us cherish and protect this precious resource,
For without it, there can be no life, no force.

Tania Winther

* Water brushstrokes, 2020, acrylic painting on canvas, 80x80 cm, Tania Winther

CONTENTS

SAVE OUR PLANET

PREFACE

In the vast expanse of our world's oceans lies an intricate and fragile ecosystem teeming with life and wonder. Yet, in recent years, the haunting reality of marine littering and ocean pollution has come to the forefront of our consciousness. The relentless assault of human activities has left an indelible mark on these once-pristine waters, threatening the very survival of countless species and jeopardizing the balance of our planet.

"Oceans of hope" is a heartfelt response to this environmental crisis, offering a profound exploration of the subject through the lens of poetry and prose. It is an earnest attempt to capture the beauty, sadness, and urgency that surrounds marine littering and ocean pollution. Through carefully woven words and evocative imagery, this collection aims to stir the depths of our emotions and awaken a sense of responsibility within us all.

Poetry has a unique power to connect us with the world around us, to speak to our hearts and minds in a way that transcends mere facts and figures. It allows us to delve into the depths of human experience and reflect upon our impact on the natural world. Within these pages, you will find a great variety of verses that blend artistry and activism, inviting contemplation and inspiring action.

As you embark on this poetic journey, prepare to confront the stark realities that lie beneath the surface. Allow the words to wash over you like the ebb and flow of the tides, their rhythmic cadence echoing the pulse of the ocean itself. Each poem serves as a call to arms, a gentle reminder of our shared responsibility to protect and preserve these vital ecosystems.

But amidst the anguish, you will also find glimmers of hope. Within these lines, we celebrate the tireless efforts of individuals, organizations, and communities who work diligently to combat marine littering and ocean pollution. Their stories serve as beacons of light, illuminating the path towards a more sustainable future.

"Oceans of hope" is not just a book; it is a plea for change, an invitation to join the chorus of voices advocating for the preservation of our oceans. It is a testament to the resilience of nature and the indomitable spirit of humanity. May it inspire us all to take action, to reevaluate our choices, and to forge a new path towards a cleaner, healthier, and more harmonious relationship with the oceans that have nurtured us since time immemorial.

With every turned page, may we come closer to understanding the magnitude of the challenge before us. May we find solace, motivation, and a renewed determination to be the guardians of our seas. Together, let us embark on this journey, for the fate of our oceans and the destiny of generations yet unborn depend on our collective efforts.

Here are some of the key problems today:

Marine Pollution poses a significant threat to the seas and marine life. It includes various forms, such as plastic debris, oil spills, chemicals, and nutrient runoff. These pollutants can harm marine ecosystems, damage coral reefs, and endanger marine species.

Overfishing: Overfishing occurs when fishing activities exceed the sustainable yield of fish populations. This practice depletes fish stocks, disrupts marine food chains, and threatens the livelihoods of communities dependent on fishing.

Coral Reef Degradation: Coral reefs, highly diverse and fragile ecosystems, are under threat due to factors like pollution, rising sea temperatures, ocean acidification, and destructive fishing practices. Their degradation has severe consequences for marine biodiversity and coastal protection.

Climate Change and Ocean Acidification: Rising greenhouse gas emissions contribute to climate change, leading to warmer sea temperatures, altered ocean currents, and sea-level rise. These changes affect marine ecosystems, including coral reefs and the distribution of marine species. Additionally, increased carbon dioxide absorption by the oceans causes ocean acidification, which can harm marine organisms.

Loss of Biodiversity: Human activities, including pollution, habitat destruction, and overfishing, have resulted in the loss of marine biodiversity. This reduction in species diversity can disrupt ecosystem balance and resilience.

Illegal, Unreported, and Unregulated (IUU) Fishing: IUU fishing refers to fishing activities conducted outside the regulations and without proper reporting. It undermines efforts to manage and conserve fish stocks, threatens sustainability, and contributes to overfishing.

Marine Habitat Destruction: Destruction and degradation of coastal habitats, such as mangroves, seagrass beds, and salt marshes, have adverse effects on marine ecosystems. These habitats provide vital breeding grounds, nurseries, and feeding areas for various marine species.

Invasive Species: The introduction of non-native species into marine ecosystems can have detrimental effects. Invasive species can outcompete native species, disrupt ecological balance, and damage habitats. It's crucial to note that the situation may have changed, and new challenges may have emerged since this poetry book has been published. Staying informed with the latest scientific research and news from reputable sources would provide more up-to-date information on the problems facing the seas today.

Scientists are continuously conducting extensive research to provide evidence of marine pollution and its detrimental effects on the environment.
Here are some examples of scientific studies and evidence related to marine pollution:

Plastic Pollution: Numerous studies have documented the presence and impact of plastic pollution in the oceans. For instance, a global estimate published in "Science today" estimated that 8 million metric tons of plastic waste enter the oceans annually. This plastic pollution can harm marine life through entanglement, ingestion, and habitat destruction.

Oil Spills: Oil spills have been a significant concern for marine ecosystems. The Deepwater Horizon oil spill in 2010, one of the largest in history, led to extensive research on its impact. Scientists have examined the effects of oil spills on marine organisms, including fish, marine mammals, and birds, as well as long-term impacts on habitats and ecosystems.

Chemical Pollution: Chemical pollutants, such as heavy metals, pesticides, and industrial chemicals, can contaminate marine environments. Scientific studies have demonstrated the toxic effects of these

pollutants on marine organisms, including reproductive issues, developmental abnormalities, and compromised immune systems.
Harmful Algal Blooms: Harmful algal blooms (HABs) are events when certain species of algae grow rapidly, producing toxins that can be harmful to marine life and human health. Researchers have extensively studied HABs and their causes, as well as the impacts on marine ecosystems, including fish kills, shellfish poisoning, and damage to coral reefs.

Microplastics: Microplastics, small plastic particles less than 5 millimeters in size, have been found in oceans worldwide. Numerous scientific studies have detected microplastics in marine organisms, including fish, shellfish, and marine mammals, raising concerns about their potential impacts on the food web and ecosystem health.
Coral Reef Degradation: Scientists have extensively studied the causes and consequences of coral reef degradation. Research has shown that factors like pollution, warming sea temperatures, ocean acidification, and destructive fishing practices contribute to coral reef decline. Coral bleaching, a phenomenon linked to rising water temperatures, has received significant attention due to its devastating impact on coral reefs worldwide.

These examples highlight some of the science regarding marine pollution and its impacts on marine ecosystems. Scientists are continuously conducting research to better understand the extent of the problem and develop strategies for mitigation and conservation. I advise you all to stay up to date and read recent research conducted on the topic. My book of poems is merely a plea for change and awareness on a crucial topic.
A topic all humans should have an interest in, to preserve our mother nature, and for our future generations.

With deepest regards,

T. WINTHER ART

Tania Winther

The water once pure and clear,
now tainted with waste and fear.
A tragedy of human design,
pollution now a scourge, a sign.
From rivers to oceans, it spreads,
the damage to our planet, it embeds.
Fish and wildlife suffer the most,
their habitats destroyed, their lives lost.
Plastic waste, oil spills, and more,
the consequences, we can't ignore.
The toxins seep into the soil,
affecting all life, from meadow to foil.
The water that once sustained us all,
now a burden, a problem, a call.
A call to action, a call to care,
to clean the waters, to be aware.
We must take responsibility,
and act with a sense of urgency.
We must save the water, our lifeline,
for the sake of humanity, for all time.
Let us come together and unite,
to make the water once again right.
Let us clean, let us heal,
and let the water once again reveal.

Tania Winther

* Ante Mortem 2014, oil painting on canvas, 20x20 cm, Liv Fjellsol. (Photo: Hege Finsrud)

Healing the wounds of habitat neglect

In the deep blue ocean, a fragile ballet,
Where marine habitats thrive in a delicate array,
But alas, a tale of destruction unfolds,
As coastal sanctuaries succumb to human molds.

Majestic mangroves, nature's fortresses on land,
With roots that entwine, a steadfast band,
They shield the coast from tempestuous tides,
Nurturing life in their watery hides.

Yet progress paves way for ambition's chase,
As axes swing, leaving barren space,
Mangroves, once thriving, now diminished and frayed,
Their absence felt in every wave's cascade.

Seagrass beds, like emerald tapestries unfurled,
Where an underwater symphony swiftly whirls,
A shelter for creatures, small and grand,
Providing refuge in their vibrant strand.

But human hands, driven by profit's lure,
Deploy destructive forces, unforgiving and sure,
Trawlers drag their nets, entwined in greed,
Decimating seagrass beds, leaving barren need.

Salt marshes, nature's guardians of the shore,
A haven for birds and countless more,
Their sturdy reeds sway in the salty breeze,
Absorbing the impact of nature's unease.

Yet the wheels of progress roll with no restraint,

Draining marshes, ignoring nature's plaint,
Once teeming with life, now a desolate plain,
Silenced whispers of creatures in mourning refrain.

Oh, marine habitat destruction, a grievous plight,
As precious ecosystems vanish from sight,
But in this somber tale, there lies a plea,
To awaken humanity's conscience and decree.

Let us halt the march of destruction's reign,
Embrace sustainable practices, break the chain,
For the marine habitats, fragile and true,
Are the essence of life, for me and for you.

Together we must rise, with hearts that yearn,
To restore what's lost, to let the ecosystems return,
For in the preservation of these habitats rare,
Lies the promise of a future, where life can repair.

So let us unite, in a chorus of resolve,
To protect marine habitats, as nature's absolve,
For only through harmony, love, and respect,
Can we heal the wounds of habitat neglect.

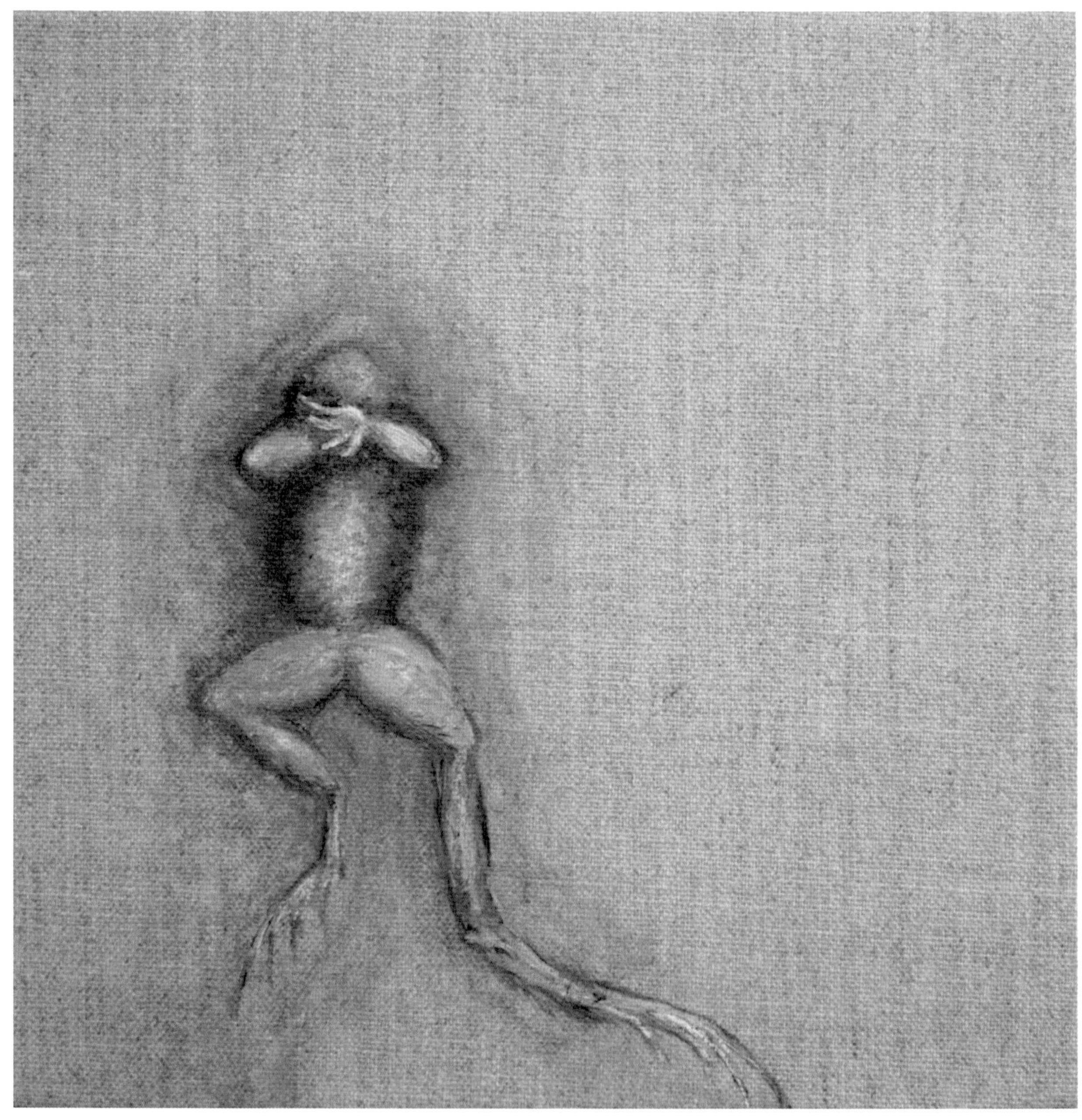

* Post Mortem, 2014, oil painting on canvas, 20x20 cm, Liv Fjellsol. (Photo: Hege Finsrud)

MARINE POLLUTION AND PLASTIC WASTE: A LOOMING THREAT TO OUR OCEANS

Introduction:
Marine pollution, especially in the form of plastic waste, has become an alarming global crisis. The unsustainable production, consumption, and disposal of plastics have resulted in widespread contamination of our oceans, posing grave threats to marine ecosystems and human well-being. This essay explores the causes, impacts, and potential solutions to the pressing issue of marine pollution and plastic waste.

The Scope of Marine Pollution:
Marine pollution encompasses a range of contaminants, including chemicals, oil spills, heavy metals, and plastic debris. Among these, plastic waste has emerged as a pervasive and persistent problem. Every year, millions of metric tons of plastic end up in the ocean, with devastating consequences for marine life, habitats, and ecosystems.

The Menace of Plastic Waste:
Plastic waste, particularly single-use plastics, has proven to be a significant contributor to marine pollution. These plastics, which take hundreds of years to decompose, accumulate in oceans, rivers, and coastlines. Plastic debris poses entanglement and ingestion risks to marine animals, leading to injury, suffocation, and death. Additionally, the breakdown of plastics into microplastics, tiny particles less than 5 millimeters in size, further exacerbates the problem. Microplastics contaminate the water column, sediments, and marine organisms, with potential implications for the entire food chain, including human consumption.

Causes of Marine Plastic Pollution:
The causes of marine plastic pollution are multifaceted. Inadequate waste management infrastructure, improper disposal practices, and limited recycling efforts contribute to plastic leakage into the environment. Irresponsible manufacturing and packaging practices, excessive consumerism, and lack of awareness further exacerbate the problem. Plastic waste generated on land often finds its way into rivers and eventually reaches the ocean through runoff or direct dumping, impacting coastal areas and remote marine habitats alike.

Impacts on Marine Ecosystems and Human Health:
Marine pollution and plastic waste have significant ecological and human health consequences. Plastic debris entangles and suffocates marine animals, disrupts their behavior, and affects reproduction and growth rates. Toxic chemicals present in plastics, such as additives and persistent organic pollutants, can leach into the water, posing risks to marine organisms and potentially entering the human food chain. The

ingestion of microplastics by marine species raises concerns about the transfer of harmful substances to humans through seafood consumption.

Addressing the Crisis: Solutions and Actions

Combating marine pollution and plastic waste requires a multi-pronged approach involving governments, industries, communities, and individuals. Some key strategies include:

Reducing plastic production and consumption: Promoting alternatives to single-use plastics, implementing plastic bag bans, and encouraging responsible consumer behavior can significantly decrease plastic waste.

Improving waste management: Investing in robust waste collection, recycling infrastructure, and proper disposal systems is crucial. Encouraging waste segregation, recycling education, and innovative recycling technologies can help reduce plastic leakage into the environment.

Promoting policy interventions: Governments must enact and enforce strict regulations on plastic production, labeling, and waste management. Extended producer responsibility programs can hold manufacturers accountable for the lifecycle of their products.

Raising awareness and education: Public campaigns and educational initiatives are essential to inform communities about the impacts of plastic pollution and promote behavioral changes. Education should target individuals, businesses, and schools to foster a culture of sustainability and responsible consumption.

Encouraging circular economy approaches: Transitioning to a circular economy model, where materials are reused, recycled, or repurposed, reduces the demand for new plastics and promotes resource efficiency.

Conclusion:

Marine pollution and plastic waste pose a severe threat to the health and resilience of our oceans. To protect marine ecosystems and ensure a sustainable future, it is imperative that we take immediate and concerted action. By reducing plastic consumption, improving waste management practices, implementing effective policies, and promoting education and awareness, we can mitigate the impacts of marine pollution and plastic waste. It is our responsibility to safeguard the health of our oceans for the well-being of marine life, ecosystems, and future generations. Together, we can work towards a cleaner and healthier marine environment.

* TITANIC, 2016, D.G.A, 42x59 cm, Knut Løvås.

Coastal marshes, a haven of serenity,
Invaders seize the opportunity with audacity.
They alter the landscape, disturb the tranquility,
Leaving behind a trail of ecological fragility.

Tania Winther

What causes Marine pollution?

In my philosophical search, I delve deep into the heart of marine pollution, seeking answers beyond the surface of mere consequences. The search unfolds as a tale of intertwined complexities, where human actions reverberate through the delicate balance of nature, leaving indelible marks on the vastness of the seas.

At the core of this search lies the human quest for progress, shaped by ambition and an insatiable hunger for convenience and consumption. As civilizations evolved, so did our capacity to harness the Earth's resources, exploiting them for our comfort and growth. The spark of industrial revolution ignited a fire of innovation, birthing a world of wonders and possibilities.

Yet, beneath the surface of this transformation lay an unintended cost—the slow erosion of harmony between humanity and nature. It was in the fervor of this transformative age that the roots of marine pollution were inadvertently sown. As industry and urbanization grew, so did the demand for cheap and disposable materials, giving birth to the age of plastic.

Plastic, seemingly a marvel of modern ingenuity, served as a potent symbol of our creative prowess. Its versatility and durability made it an indispensable tool in shaping the world around us. However, its permanence in the natural world belied its transient utility. As plastic waste found its way into the oceans, the true cost of our convenience began to manifest.

Further in my search I saw where human values and attitudes intertwined with economic interests and cultural norms. A sense of detachment from nature emerged, as oceans came to be seen as vast voids—a limitless expanse to discard waste without thought or consequence.

In the pursuit of economic growth, short-sighted decisions often prevailed, prioritizing profit over preservation. Industries sought to cut costs, and waste disposal practices often disregarded environmental impact. This revealed a paradox—the very waters that nurtured life were, in turn, tainted by human greed and disregard for the interconnectedness of all things.

Moreover, my search whispered the tale of unbridled consumption, where consumer culture glorified disposability and excess. Single-use items became emblematic of modern convenience, saturating every aspect of daily life. The allure of immediacy overshadowed the foresight to consider the long-term repercussions.

Yet, within this intricate search, glimmers of hope shimmered like moonlight on the waves. My search illuminated the potential for change—a call to reevaluate our values and embrace a philosophy of sustainable coexistence. Just as our actions had unwittingly caused marine pollution, so too could our conscious choices be the catalyst for transformation.

It became evident that the solution lay not solely in regulations or technological advancements but in a fundamental shift in our collective consciousness. The seas, once relegated to a distant realm beyond human responsibility, emerged as mirrors reflecting our deepest virtues and vices.

A reconnection with nature and a reverence for the oceans beckoned us towards a new chapter—in search of harmony, where human progress could coexist in symbiosis with ecological balance. Embracing the philosophic notion of interconnectedness, we understood that what transpires in the depths of the oceans echoes through every aspect of our lives.

Through this philosophicum search of mine, the root causes of marine pollution emerged as the sum of our choices—the collective consequences of human values, actions, and aspirations. It urged us to ponder our role in the grand collectiveness of existence, encouraging a harmonious dance with nature's rhythm rather than a discordant battle for dominance.

My search for the cause of marine pollution, when viewed through the lens of philosophy, became a profound exploration of my journey—a conscious reflection and a new urge for collective action to shape the world's course. It challenged us to transcend the boundaries of our own existence, embracing a broader understanding of our place within the interconnected web of life.

RIDDLE

Amidst the emerald canopy's sway,
A riddle of our world holds sway.
In hues of blue and vibrant green,
A puzzle, profound and unseen.

I thrive upon the desert's sand,
Yet, my water's slipping from my hand.
My breath sustains the living Earth,
But heed my call for I'm in dearth.

Once a carpet, lush and vast,
Now a canvas, scarred and cast.
My lungs once clear, now choking air,
A plea for change, a heartfelt prayer.

What am I?

*Answer: I am the environment.

DYSTOPIAN WORLD

In this dystopian world, where hope seems remote,
The ocean's plight a haunting anecdote,
The waves once lustrous, now tainted and marred,
By the plastic waves, a relentless barrage.

The seafloor, a graveyard of discarded dreams,
Where life once thrived in vibrant, vibrant streams,
Now suffocated, entangled in plastic's snare,
Creatures silenced, burdened by despair.

The mighty whales, majestic and grand,
Their songs silenced by the plastic demand,
Their colossal bodies bear the scars,
Of humanity's negligence, its callous disregard.

The turtles, once wise, navigating the tides,
Now struggle against currents, plastic collides,
Their gentle hearts broken by our human greed,
As they mistake plastic for life-sustaining feed.

The coral reefs, once vibrant and alive,
Now bleached and barren, no longer thrive,
A pale reminder of nature's fragile grace,
Submerged in plastic waste, a tragic embrace.

But in this bleak landscape, a flicker of hope,
A collective awakening, a chance to cope,
For in the depths of despair, a seed is sown,
A determination to reclaim what is known.

With every mindful step, every conscious choice,
We can stem the plastic tide, find a new voice,

By reducing, recycling, and choosing with care,
We can heal the ocean, its life we can repair.

Let's forge a path towards a world pristine,
Where the ocean's depths once again gleam,
A future where plastic's reign is undone,
And life in the sea can forever run.

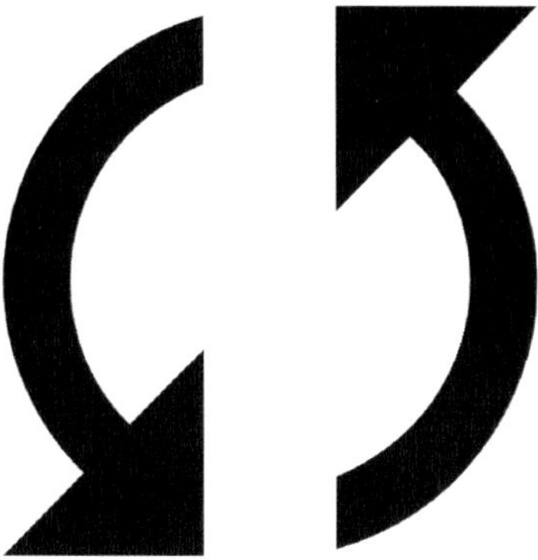

* Photo by Linda Kristiansen. 2018 (Part of her series of a dystopian "Plastic World".)

How to stop pollution?

Stopping plastic pollution demands a multifaceted approach that involves collective action from individuals, governments, industries, and organizations. While it may be a complex challenge, here are some key strategies to help combat plastic pollution:

Reduce Single-Use Plastics: Encourage the use of alternatives to single-use plastics such as reusable bags, bottles, and containers. Embrace a culture of sustainability by making conscious choices to minimize plastic waste in daily life.

Promote Recycling and Proper Disposal: Establish and enforce effective recycling programs, ensuring that plastic waste is collected, sorted, and processed responsibly. Educate communities about proper disposal methods to prevent plastic from entering waterways.

Encourage Innovation: Support research and development of biodegradable plastics and eco-friendly packaging alternatives. Embrace technology and innovation to find sustainable solutions that reduce the environmental impact of plastic.

Raise Awareness: Educate the public about the consequences of plastic pollution on marine life and ecosystems. Foster a sense of environmental responsibility and empower individuals to take action.

Implement Bans and Regulations: Advocate for government policies that ban or restrict the use of single-use plastics, such as plastic bags, straws, and Styrofoam containers. Enforce strict regulations on industrial discharge and littering.

Clean-Up Initiatives: Organize and participate in beach clean-up drives and community-led efforts to remove plastic waste from shorelines and water bodies. Engage volunteers and local communities in these initiatives.

Corporate Responsibility: Encourage businesses to adopt sustainable practices and reduce plastic usage in their operations. Hold corporations accountable for their plastic waste and promote eco-friendly packaging.

International Collaboration: Foster cooperation between nations to address the global nature of plastic pollution. Promote international agreements and initiatives to combat marine litter.

Support NGOs and Research: Contribute to and support organizations that work towards combating plastic pollution. Fund research projects focused on understanding and mitigating plastic's impact on the environment.

Education and Advocacy: Engage in advocacy efforts to push for stronger environmental policies and raise awareness among policymakers, influencers, and the general public about the urgency of addressing plastic pollution.

By integrating these strategies into our collective efforts, we can take significant steps towards mitigating plastic pollution and fostering a sustainable relationship with the oceans and the planet as a whole. Remember that every small action counts, and together, we can create a future where plastic pollution is but a chapter in our past.

Even though your contribution may be just a tiny drop in the vast sea.
One drop leads to two.
That leads to more.

* Photo by Linda Kristiansen, 2018 (Part of her series of a dystopian "Plastic World".)

Invasive species, a battle we wage,
To safeguard the oceans, turn a new page.
With determination and collaborative might,
We can protect marine ecosystems in their full might.

Tania Winther

* Slowly drowning, 2017, Drawing, 20x30 cm, Tania Winther

SILENT SCREAMS

In a dystopian realm where shadows prevail,
Where the ocean's soul has been engulfed by a plastic veil,
A tragic tale unfolds of nature's precious grace,
Lamentations echo in this desolate place.

Once teeming with life, the sea's vibrant embrace,
Now plagued by the remnants of our wasteful embrace,
Mountains of plastic rise, suffocating the waves,
Silent screams of creatures lost in watery graves.

The coral reefs, once a kaleidoscope of hues,
Now bleached and lifeless, forgotten and abused,
The vibrant fish that danced in the currents so free,
Now swim through a graveyard, surrounded by debris.

Sea turtles, majestic, their journeys cut short,
Entangled in discarded nets, a twisted consort,
The dolphins and whales, their songs now suppressed,
Muffling cries for help in a world so distressed.

The seabirds, once soaring with grace in the skies,
Now with stomachs full of plastic, their beauty belies,
Their wings heavy with burden, their spirits held down,
A symphony of sorrow, a mournful sound.

Oh, what have we done, in our reckless pursuit,
For convenience and profit, our values gone mute,
The ocean, once bountiful, a source of life's flow,
Now a graveyard of dreams, a symbol of woe.

But amidst this despair, a glimmer of light,
A call to action, to set things right,
To mend our mistakes and heal the wounds we've caused,
To restore the balance and give nature's voice applause.

For the power lies within us, to rewrite the script,
To reclaim the ocean's essence, from its dystopian grip,
Let's unite in our efforts, for a world that can be,
Where plastic's reign ends, and life can flourish, free.

* Photo by Linda Kristiansen, 2018 (Part of her series of a dystopian "Plastic World".)

Invisible invaders, they silently spread,
Outcompeting natives, leaving them in dread.
They multiply swiftly, their populations soar,
Disrupting the balance that thrived before.

Tania Winther

* Recovery, 2022, acrylic painting on canvas, 120x60 cm, Liv Fjellsol. (Photo: Hege Finsrud)

SAD HAIKU

Plastic taints the shore,
Ocean's plea for cleaner days,
Marine life weeps on.

Seabirds tangled, trapped,
Garbage chokes their fragile wings,
Marine litter's toll.

Beaches stained with waste,
Tide unveils mankind's debris,
Ocean's cry for change.

Plastic islands drift,
Seas suffocated by waste,
Marine life in pain.

Nature's tears well up,
Littered waves reflect our sins,
Heal the ocean's heart.

Tangled nets and lines,
Sea creatures entwined in death,
Litter's deadly grasp.

Plastic fragments float,
Invisible menace lurks,
Marine life endangered.

Turtles mistake bags,
For jellyfish, fatal feast,
Litter's cruel deceit.

Beacons of hope rise,
Cleanup efforts shape new tides,
Rescue from litter.

Sunset hues reveal,
Trash-strewn shores, a bitter truth,
Marine litter's scar.

Seashells now cradle,
Microplastics, silent harm,
Litter's toxic reach.

Children's laughter fades,
As polluted waves crash down,
Marine future bleak.

With each mindful step,
We can cleanse the ocean's wounds,
Litter's end in sight.

Awakened conscience,
Restoring purity and grace,
Marine litter's end.

Gentle ocean breeze,
Whispers of a cleaner world,
Marine litter's end.

Hands joined in purpose,
Clearing shores, united strength,
Litter's grip released.

Seeds of change take root,
Education blooms anew,
Marine litter's foe.

* A.I generated.

The perils of overfishing and illegal unreported fishing a global crisis & a threat to sustainable fisheries?

Introduction:
Overfishing has emerged as a pressing global issue the last 50 years, threatening the delicate balance of marine ecosystems and endangering the livelihoods of millions of people who depend on the ocean for sustenance. This short text explores the problems associated with overfishing, including ecological imbalances, the depletion of fish stocks, and the socio-economic consequences.
Illegal, Unreported, and Unregulated (IUU) fishing has emerged as a significant global concern, undermining efforts to achieve sustainable fisheries and threatening the health of marine ecosystems. This essay delves into the causes and consequences of IUU fishing, highlighting its environmental, economic, and social impacts, as well as the need for robust international cooperation to combat this illicit practice.
Ecological Imbalances:
Overfishing disrupts the intricate life in marine ecosystems, leading to severe ecological imbalances. Removing a significant portion of fish populations disrupts the predator-prey relationships, causing a ripple effect throughout the food chain. The absence of top predators, such as sharks, leads to an explosion in prey species, affecting the abundance and diversity of other organisms. Furthermore, the loss of herbivorous fish, such as parrotfish, contributes to the degradation of coral reefs as they are unable to control algae growth. These imbalances have cascading effects on the health and resilience of marine habitats.

Understanding IUU Fishing:
IUU fishing encompasses a range of activities that violate national and international fishing laws and regulations. It involves fishing without proper authorization, exceeding catch limits, using prohibited gear, engaging in destructive practices, and operating in areas protected for conservation purposes. IUU fishing often occurs in remote or poorly regulated regions, exploiting weak governance and enforcement systems.

Depletion of Fish Stocks:
The unrelenting pursuit of fish has resulted in the depletion of numerous fish stocks worldwide. Unsustainable fishing practices, including the use of large-scale industrial fishing vessels, destructive fishing gear, and illegal fishing, have pushed many species to the brink of collapse. Some iconic fish populations, such as cod, tuna, and salmon, have experienced dramatic declines due to overfishing. The loss of these key species not only disrupts ecosystems but also threatens the global food security and the livelihoods of fishing communities.

Socio-Economic Consequences:

Overfishing has far-reaching socio-economic consequences, affecting both coastal communities and global markets. Small-scale and artisanal fishermen, who rely on fish as their primary source of income, face dwindling catches, economic instability, and even displacement. These communities often lack alternative livelihood options, leading to poverty and social unrest. Moreover, the economic impact extends to the wider population, as the fishing industry supports numerous jobs in processing, distribution, and tourism. The collapse of fish stocks disrupts supply chains, leading to higher prices, unemployment, and market instability.

Economic Consequences:

IUU fishing undermines the economic sustainability of legitimate fisheries. It distorts markets by flooding them with illegal, cheaply caught fish, reducing the profitability of legal operations. Small-scale fishermen and coastal communities, who rely on fishing for their livelihoods, suffer the most. The depletion of fish stocks due to IUU fishing leads to reduced catches and income, increased poverty, and potential displacement of local communities. Furthermore, it hampers efforts to develop sustainable fisheries management practices, hindering long-term economic growth and food security.

Social Implications:

The social impacts of IUU fishing are multifaceted. It jeopardizes the rights and well-being of small-scale fishermen and coastal communities, who often lack the resources and capacity to compete with illegal operators. IUU fishing can fuel conflicts between artisanal and industrial fishing fleets, exacerbating tensions over access to resources. Additionally, it perpetuates labor rights abuses, including human trafficking and forced labor, as vulnerable individuals are exploited on IUU fishing vessels.

International Cooperation and Solutions:

Addressing IUU fishing requires a multifaceted approach, including robust international cooperation, effective monitoring and enforcement systems, and capacity building in developing countries. Governments and relevant stakeholders must strengthen legal frameworks and improve information sharing to detect and prosecute IUU fishing activities. International agreements, such as the Port State Measures Agreement and regional fisheries management organizations, play a crucial role in harmonizing regulations, promoting sustainable practices, and facilitating collaboration among nations.

Technological advancements, such as satellite tracking and vessel monitoring systems, can enhance surveillance and monitoring capabilities, enabling authorities to detect and deter IUU fishing. Improved traceability and certification schemes for seafood products help ensure the legality and sustainability of fishery supply chains. Raising consumer awareness and promoting sustainable seafood choices also play a vital role in reducing the demand for illegally caught fish.

Environmental Impacts:

Beyond the immediate effects on fish populations, overfishing contributes to broader environmental concerns. Destructive fishing practices, such as bottom trawling and dynamite fishing, damage marine habitats, including coral reefs and seafloor ecosystems. These practices also result in bycatch, where non-target species, including marine mammals, sea turtles, and seabirds, are unintentionally caught and killed. Overfishing also contributes to ocean pollution through discarded fishing gear, including nets and lines, which entangle marine life and persist as marine debris.

IUU fishing poses significant environmental threats. Irresponsible fishing practices, such as bottom trawling and dynamite fishing, cause habitat destruction, leading to the degradation of marine ecosystems, including coral reefs and seafloor habitats. Overfishing of target species and high levels of bycatch result in population declines and imbalances, disrupting food chains and reducing biodiversity. IUU fishing also contributes to the introduction of invasive species, further destabilizing ecosystems.

Conclusion:
The problems associated with overfishing demand urgent attention and concerted global efforts. Sustainable fishing practices, such as implementing fishing quotas, regulating fishing gear, and establishing marine protected areas, are essential for restoring fish populations and promoting ecosystem resilience. International collaboration, stricter enforcement of fishing regulations, and consumer awareness and support for sustainably sourced seafood are crucial steps in addressing the overfishing crisis. By taking action now, we can safeguard our oceans, preserve marine biodiversity, and secure the livelihoods of future generations. Illegal, Unreported, and Unregulated (IUU) fishing undermines the integrity of global fisheries, depletes fish stocks, damages marine ecosystems, and threatens the livelihoods of millions of people worldwide. The fight against IUU fishing requires collective action, commitment, and collaboration among governments, international organizations, and stakeholders at all levels. By implementing effective monitoring and enforcement mechanisms, strengthening governance, and promoting sustainable practices, we can safeguard the future of our oceans, protect vulnerable communities, and preserve marine biodiversity for generations to come.

* A.I. generated.

The Sapphire Tides

Beneath the waves, a vibrant world of life,
Now colored by our greed, our endless strife.
In moments lost to time, we chose to blind,
To nature's plea, our hearts were unaligned.

The sapphire tides once sang a soothing song,
Now suffocate, as plastic waves prolong.
With every passing day, the ocean cries,
Her ancient wisdom drowned by human lies.

What have we done, in our relentless quest?
To satiate desires, we failed the test.
We poisoned seas with reckless disregard,
The consequences grave, now hit us hard.

As time casts its melancholic hue,
The sea creatures, they whisper tales anew.
Of coral reefs that weep in silent woe,
Of fish entangled, struggling to grow.

The albatross, a graceful, ghostly sight,
With stomachs full of plastic day and night.
Our refuse haunts their nests, their young, their skies,
No sanctuary left for them to rise.

In vast expanse, where waves meet the shore,
We witness tragedy that we ignore.
The beaches wear a plastic-laden shroud,
Our legacy, a burial wrapped in plastic proud.

Yet, even in despair, hope's light remains,
If only we could learn from nature's strains.
To mend our ways and steer a different way,

Before the ocean's heart loses its force.

Let's halt the flow of plastic's deadly dance,
Embrace sustainable steps, give Earth a chance.
The time has come to heal, to reunite,
With nature's rhythm, to make the world right.

* The Sapphire Tides, 2021, Mixed Media, Spray paint & Acrylics, 50 x 70 cm, Tania Winther.

THINK
GREEN

HAIKU OF THE SEAS

Azure expanse roars,
Whispers of ancient secrets,
Ocean's timeless song.

Crested waves crash down,
Serenade of salty breeze,
Sea's eternal dance.

Gulls soar in the sky,
Salt spray kisses sun-kissed cheeks,
Seascape's endless charm.

Beneath the surface,
Coral blooms in vibrant hues,
Hidden wonders thrive.

Footprints in the sand,
Tide's embrace, forever changed,
Sea's eternal shift.

Majestic tides roar,
Whispers of untold stories,
Sea's vast mystery.

Seashells on the shore,
Echoes of forgotten tales,
Ocean's memoirs found.

Golden sunset paints,
Horizon kissed by the sea,
Nature's masterpiece.

Sailboats on the horizon,
Guided by the dancing waves,
Sea's gentle guidance.

Crashing waves retreat,
Leaving traces of solace,
Serenity found.

Whispering seagrass,
Caressed by the ocean's breath,
Sea's lullaby calls.

Crystal drops cascade,
Life's essence, pure and vital,
Water's gift, revered.

Whispering river,
Flowing through ancient valleys,
Life's sustenance flows.

Raindrops on petals,
Nature's delicate touch,
Water's gentle grace.

Mighty waterfall,
Power unleashed, roaring force,
Water's strength revealed.

Dew on morning grass,
Nature's jewels shimmering,
Water's tender touch.

Ocean's vast expanse,
Endless depths and mysteries,
Water's vast embrace.

* Healing waves, 2021, acrylic on canvas, 50x70 cm, Tania Winther.

Ode to the Cries of Marine Life

Ode to the cries of marine life,
Silenced by plastic's merciless strife,
In the depths of the ocean's vast embrace,
A silent destruction, an invisible trace.

Oh, the wails that echo through the waves,
As plastic infiltrates their watery graves,
The dolphins, once playful, now entangled,
Their freedom ensnared, their spirits strangled.

The gentle sea turtles, ancient and wise,
Seek solace in waters where plastic lies,
Mistaking bags for nourishing prey,
Their fate sealed by a tragic display.

Majestic whales, rulers of the sea,
Their mournful songs, a plea to be free,
Ensnared by ghost nets and debris so vast,
Their melodies stifled, their future surpassed.

Beneath the surface, a fragile ballet,
Microplastics dance, unseen but at play,
Tiny particles infiltrate their being,
A toxic invasion, their very core fleeing.

The coral reefs, once vibrant and alive,
Now bleached and suffocated, unable to thrive,
The intricate ecosystems they once sustained,
Now bear witness to a world deeply pained.

Oh, the silent destruction, a tragedy untold,
As plastic pollution takes its stronghold,
But let these cries of the silenced sea,
Ignite a fire within us to set them free.

Let us stand as guardians, voices so strong,
Demanding change, righting the wrong,
For the cries of marine life must be heard,

Their future preserved, their voices restored.

In unity we rise, hearts intertwined,
To heal the ocean, one step at a time,
For it is our duty, a solemn decree,
To safeguard the seas and set life free.

Let this ode be a rallying call,
To halt the destruction, to break the fall,
And together we'll rewrite this tragic tale,
Where marine life's cries no longer wail.

* Coral Society, 2023, acrylic on canvas, 100x80cm, Mariel Mikalsen.

THE PRECARIOUS STATE OF CORAL REEFS: AN URGENT CALL FOR CONSERVATION

Introduction:
Coral reefs, vibrant underwater ecosystems teeming with life, are facing an unprecedented crisis. These delicate and diverse habitats, often referred to as the "rainforests of the sea," are under immense threat due to human activities and environmental stressors. This essay delves into the current situation of coral reefs, the causes of their decline, and the urgent need for conservation measures.

The State of Coral Reefs:
Coral reefs are home to a staggering array of marine life, providing shelter, feeding grounds, and breeding sites for countless species. They cover a mere 0.2% of the ocean's surface but support about 25% of all marine organisms. However, alarming statistics reveal a grim reality. It is estimated that more than 30% of coral reefs worldwide have already been destroyed, and an additional 60% are under significant threat. The Great Barrier Reef, the largest coral reef ecosystem, has experienced substantial bleaching events, leading to widespread coral mortality.

Causes of Decline:
Several factors contribute to the decline of coral reefs, the most prominent being climate change. Rising ocean temperatures, primarily driven by greenhouse gas emissions, have led to coral bleaching, a phenomenon where corals expel the symbiotic algae that provide them with nutrients and vibrant colors. Bleached corals are more susceptible to disease and mortality, causing widespread devastation. Ocean acidification, another consequence of increased carbon dioxide absorption by the oceans, hinders the growth and development of coral reefs, making them more vulnerable to other stressors.

Human activities also pose significant threats to coral reefs. Overfishing disrupts the balance of reef ecosystems, removing key species that help maintain the health of corals. Destructive fishing practices, such as dynamite fishing and cyanide fishing, directly damage coral structures. Coastal development, pollution from agriculture and industry, and sedimentation from deforestation and land erosion further degrade coral reefs, causing smothering and reducing light penetration vital for coral growth.

The Importance of Coral Reefs:
Coral reefs play a vital role in supporting coastal communities and the global ecosystem. They act as natural barriers, protecting coastlines from storms and erosion. Coral reefs are also a source of food and livelihood for millions of people, particularly in developing countries reliant on fishing and tourism. Additionally, they contribute to the economy through revenue generated by diving and snorkeling tourism. Furthermore, coral reefs harbor potential medical breakthroughs, with organisms within them providing compounds used in the development of medicines.

The Urgent Need for Conservation:

Given the critical state of coral reefs, immediate and decisive action is imperative. Conservation efforts must prioritize the reduction of greenhouse gas emissions to mitigate climate change. International agreements, such as the Paris Agreement, play a vital role in achieving this. Local and global initiatives should focus on sustainable fishing practices, the establishment of marine protected areas, and the reduction of pollution and sedimentation from coastal development.

Public awareness and education are paramount in promoting conservation. Individuals can make a difference by supporting sustainable seafood choices, reducing their carbon footprint, and participating in coral reef restoration projects. Collaboration between governments, scientists, conservation organizations, and local communities is essential to implement effective strategies and policies for reef preservation.

Conclusion:
The plight of coral reefs demands immediate attention and concerted efforts to ensure their survival. By addressing the root causes of their decline and implementing robust conservation measures, we can protect these invaluable ecosystems and safeguard the myriad of benefits they provide. The fate of coral reefs rests in our hands, and it is our responsibility to act decisively and protect these precious habitats for future generations.

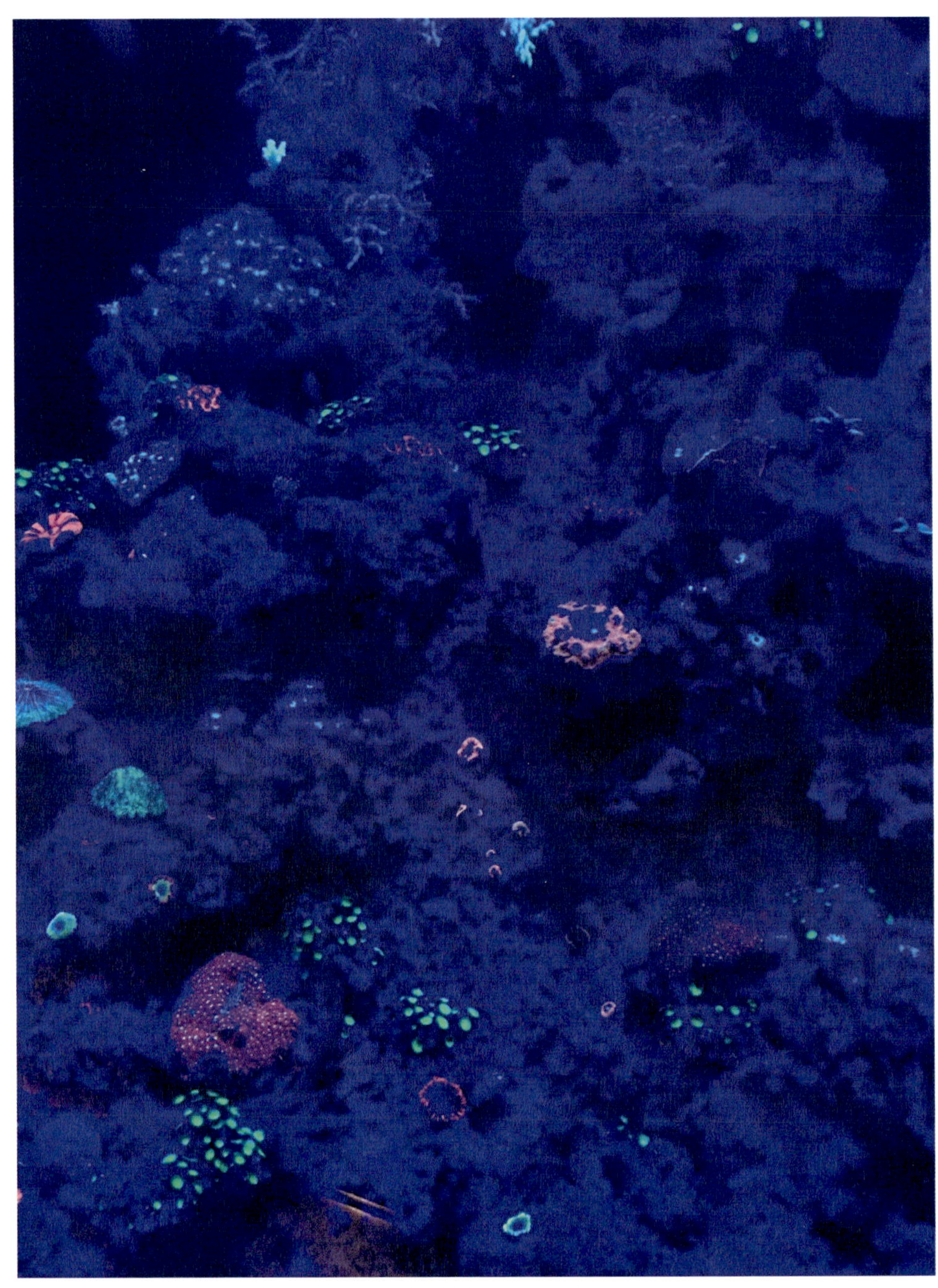

* The Deep Blue Corals, 2016, photo by Tania Winther.

AN ODE TO THE HEROES: THE ORGANIZATIONS AND COMMUNITIES WHO WORK DILIGENTLY TO COMBAT MARINE LITTERING AND OCEAN POLLUTION.

Hark! Let us sing of the champions bold,
Whose hearts are dedicated, steadfast and bold.
In the face of ocean's sorrow and plight,
They rise with courage to protect the marine's light.

Oh, ye organizations, beacons of hope,
Guiding us forward on this challenging slope.
With unwavering passion and tireless might,
You battle the perils that mar the ocean's sight.

From coast to coast, your efforts abound,
Cleaning beaches, rallying communities around.
Through cleanup campaigns, you mobilize,
Uniting hands to reclaim the ocean's skies.

In classrooms and forums, you educate,
Spreading knowledge to eradicate the toxic state.
Raising awareness, igniting the flame,
To combat littering, pollution's wicked game.

Innovators and scientists, pioneers of change,
You seek solutions in a world deranged.
Developing technologies, novel and sound,
To tackle the crisis, to turn it around.

Artists and creatives, your talents inspire,
Using your craft to ignite a fire.
Through visual expressions and storytelling might,
You awaken consciousness, shining a light.

Communities united, forging a bond,
Together, you rise, so incredibly strong.
Cleanup drives and sustainable choices,
Transforming the seas with hopeful voices.

To all who devote their hearts and hands,
To heal the oceans, protect its sands,
We sing your praises, we hold you dear,
For your dedication, we cheer and cheer.

For it is in your tireless endeavor,
That the oceans find solace, now and forever.
May your work inspire, may it never cease,
As we strive for a world where oceans find peace.

So let us raise our voices high and strong,
In honor of those who fight the ocean's wrong.
With gratitude and admiration, let us sing,
To the heroes of the sea, our eternal offering.

* Breeze, 2021, acrylic on canvas,50x70 cm, Tania Winther.

FOR THE OCEAN

The sun casts its golden rays upon the vast expanse of the ocean, once a cradle of life and tranquility. But beneath the shimmering surface lies a heartbreaking tale of devastation. Ocean pollution and marine littering have cast their dark shadows upon this once pristine realm, leaving behind a trail of destruction.

With each passing day, human activities unleash a torrent of waste into the waters. Plastic, that silent intruder, has become an unwelcome guest, infiltrating the deepest depths and desecrating the fragile ecosystems that call the ocean home. Its unnatural permanence clashes with the ever-changing rhythm of nature, trapping marine creatures in a web of entanglement and suffocation.

Imagine, if you will, the graceful dance of a majestic sea turtle, its sleek silhouette gliding through the currents. But now, picture it ensnared in a discarded fishing net, struggling desperately for freedom. The cries of distress go unheard, lost amidst the vastness of the ocean, as this symbol of resilience becomes a casualty of our negligence.

The coral reefs, once vibrant layers of color, now bear witness to our carelessness. Their delicate structures are smothered by sediment and choked by chemical pollutants. The homes of countless marine species crumble, their inhabitants left adrift in search of a sanctuary that may no longer exist. The haunting silence that echoes through these ravaged reefs is a testament to the magnitude of our impact.

And what of the marine life that unwittingly ingests our toxic offerings? A feast of plastic debris, mistaken for sustenance, fills their bellies. Birds, fish, and mammals suffer silently as their bodies become graveyards for our discarded waste. The consequences reverberate throughout the food chain, reaching even the shores where our footsteps tread.

Yet, amidst this gloom, a glimmer of hope emerges. The waves of change are slowly but surely gathering strength. Individuals, communities, and organizations unite, driven by a shared sense of responsibility. Cleanup efforts sweep across coastlines, and awareness campaigns ignite a flame of consciousness within our collective soul.

As we stand at the precipice of a defining moment, we must recognize the urgency that lingers in the air. It is not enough to mourn the desolation; action is the currency of redemption. We must reduce, reuse, and recycle, steering our choices towards a sustainable path. Innovation must guide our footsteps, seeking alternatives to single-use plastics and embracing eco-friendly practices.

For the ocean, this battered sanctuary of life, still holds within its depths the resilience to heal. Let us be the custodians it so desperately needs, guardians of its majesty. Let our actions speak louder than the tides, as we work tirelessly to restore what has been lost, to mend the wounds we have inflicted.

May we find solace in the knowledge that change is within our grasp. The ocean's plea for mercy resonates within our hearts, beckoning us to rise above the waves of apathy. Together, let us rewrite the narrative, transforming the tale of devastation into one of triumph—a testament to the power of human compassion and the enduring spirit of the ocean.

* Into the void, 2023, acrylic on canvas, 50x70 cm, Tania Winther.

The Mighty Sea

The mighty sea, oh how it roars,
With waves that crash upon the shores,
Its endless depths hold secrets untold,
Stories of adventure, both new and old.

The sea, it beckons, with its siren's call,
Drawing us in, one and all,
The salty spray upon our skin,
As we venture out, where the waves begin.

The creatures that dwell beneath the waves,
Are more mysterious than we can say,
From the smallest fish to the largest whale,
They all have a story to tell.

The sea, it can be calm and serene,
A tranquil sight, like none you've seen,
But in a flash, it can turn wild,
A force to be reckoned with, untamed and wild.

So, let us respect the mighty sea,
And all the wonders that it holds for free,
For though we may sail upon its surface,
Its true depths remain forever enigmatic and mysterious.

* Guardians of the oceans, 2017, Charcoal, 42x59 cm, Tania Winther.

Guardians of the Oceans.

In the depths where wonders lie,
Beneath the azure, endless sky,
A tale of harmony unfolds,
Where the ocean's story is told.

Where turquoise waves caress the shore,
And seagulls dance, forevermore,
Lies a fragile world, pristine and grand,
A realm we must strive to understand.

Oh, behold the mighty ocean's grace,
A cradle of life, a sacred space,
Teeming with creatures, diverse and free,
From coral reefs to the depths of the sea.

Yet, upon its surface, a somber sight,
A plea for change, a call for light,
For the tides carry more than they seem,
Whispers of a future, bound by a dream.

Sustainability, our compass true,
To navigate these waters blue,
Let's mend the wounds that we have made,
And safeguard the treasures that won't fade.

Let's weave a tapestry of hope and care,
For every creature dwelling there,
Embrace the rhythm of nature's song,
And right the balance that's been wronged.

From plastic shores to polluted seas,
Our actions ripple with each gentle breeze,
For it's in our hands to make amends,
To heal the wounds that time transcends.

Let's join our voices, hearts entwined,
To protect this jewel we've been assigned,
For when we nurture, the ocean thrives,
A testament to our love, our lives.

So, let us be stewards, strong and bold,
Guardians of the ocean's fold,
For in its depths, our destiny lies,
A sustainable future, where hope never dies.

* Guardians of the oceans II, 2017, Charcoal, 42x59 cm, Tania Winther.

RIDDLE 2

In the depths of azure realms, I dwell,
My kingdom once a vibrant spell.
But now, a riddle casts its pall,
In plastic's grip, I gasp and sprawl.

My shell, a fortress, strong and bright,
Now entangled in plastic's blight.
With every wave that crashes in,
My fate entwined, a tale of sin.

The corals dance in colors bold,
Yet, pollution's grip, they cannot hold.
Once teeming life beneath the foam,
Now plastic's shadow, I call home.

With fins that glide, I roam the seas,
Yet, plastic waste clings to me.
From ocean depths to shores afar,
I bear the scars of manmade tar.

What am I, once free and wild,
Now captive to plastic's guile?
Seek my rescue, heed my plight,
And mend the seas with caring light.

What am I?

*I am the marine animal trapped in marine pollution

* Sea Angels, 2019, D.G.A, (Digitally drawn, "Coral painter") Tania Winther.

Sea Angels

Sea angels, also referred to as sea butterflies, are a group of gelatinous sea snails that exhibit a remarkable array of adaptations for life in the open ocean. They possess delicate, transparent bodies, adorned with wing-like structures, which enable them to glide gracefully through the water. Despite their diminutive size, these ethereal creatures have a significant impact on marine ecosystems and serve as indicators of environmental health.

Biological Significance:
The Sea Angels' biology is a remarkable feat of evolution, characterized by their unique locomotion, feeding mechanisms, and reproduction strategies. Their wing-like appendages, known as parapodia, enable them to move in a rhythmic, butterfly-like manner, propelling them through the water column. Through their meticulously evolved body structures, they have adapted to exploit the rich resources found in various marine habitats.

Sea Angels exhibit a diverse range of feeding strategies, some of which involve filtering tiny phytoplankton and zooplankton from the water column using specialized feeding appendages. Their role as voracious predators of small organisms helps to regulate plankton populations, contributing to the balance and stability of marine food webs.

Reproduction and Life Cycle:
The reproductive strategies of Sea Angels are equally intriguing. They employ various mechanisms for fertilization, including internal fertilization and the deposition of egg masses. The eggs develop into free-swimming larvae, which undergo metamorphosis before reaching their adult form. The complex reproductive behaviors and life cycle patterns of these organisms have provided valuable insights into the evolutionary processes governing their survival and diversification.

Ecological Significance:
Sea Angels inhabit diverse marine environments worldwide, from polar seas to tropical waters. They are especially prevalent in regions where nutrient upwelling occurs, serving as a crucial link between primary producers and higher trophic levels. Furthermore, their sensitivity to environmental changes, such as ocean acidification and warming, makes them important bioindicators of climate change impacts on marine ecosystems.

* Arielia, 2020, D.G.A, (Digitally drawn, "Coral painter") Tania Winther

The story about Arielia

Once upon a time, in the vast open ocean, there existed a hidden realm of enchantment. This magical world was home to an extraordinary species known as Sea Angels. These ethereal creatures, with their delicate, transparent bodies and graceful movements, captivated the hearts and imaginations of all who encountered them.

In this underwater kingdom, a young Sea Angel named Arielia dreamed of exploring beyond the borders of her familiar surroundings. Unlike her companions, Arielia possessed an insatiable curiosity that propelled her to venture into uncharted waters. She yearned to discover the secrets hidden beneath the shimmering surface and to unravel the mysteries of her own existence.

Driven by her longing for adventure, Arielia embarked on a journey that took her far from her birthplace. Along the way, she encountered a vibrant array of marine life: schools of colorful fish dancing in synchrony, coral reefs adorned with intricate patterns, and majestic whales gliding through the depths. Each encounter filled her heart with awe and wonder.

As she traveled deeper into the ocean's embrace, Arielia stumbled upon a hidden realm illuminated by bioluminescent creatures. Their radiant glow transformed the darkness into a mesmerizing spectacle, casting a magical spell upon everything it touched. Entranced by the ethereal beauty, Arielia couldn't help but join the glowing ballet of lights, twirling and spiraling in harmony with her newfound companions.

During her exploration, Arielia also witnessed the intricate balance of life in the ocean. She observed the delicate dance between predator and prey, the symbiotic relationships between species, and the relentless force of nature. Through these experiences, she came to appreciate the interconnectedness of all living beings and the importance of preserving their fragile habitats.

Arielia's journey eventually led her to a remote corner of the ocean, where she stumbled upon a community of Sea Angels unlike any she had ever encountered. They possessed a unique ability to emit a radiant iridescence, painting the surrounding waters with shimmering hues. They welcomed Arielia with open arms, recognizing her adventurous spirit and her deep love for the ocean.

As the days turned into weeks and weeks into months, Arielia immersed herself in the daily lives of her newfound companions. Together, they embarked on daring escapades, exploring hidden caves, and discovering hidden treasures. They shared laughter and joy, as well as moments of introspection and reflection.

But Arielia's heart remained restless, and she knew that her destiny lay beyond the borders of this secluded haven. With a mixture of gratitude and longing, she bid farewell to her beloved community of Sea Angels, vowing to protect and preserve their enchanting home.

Returning to the vast expanse of the open ocean, Arielia continued her quest for knowledge and adventure. Along the way, she encountered other sea creatures, forging unlikely friendships and exchanging stories of their respective realms. Through her wanderings, Arielia became an ambassador for the ocean, spreading awareness of its beauty, fragility, and the urgent need for its conservation.

As time went on, Arielia's name became synonymous with courage, curiosity, and a deep love for the ocean. Her journey inspired countless others to explore, appreciate, and protect the marine world. Her legacy as a Sea Angel resonated far and wide, ensuring that the mysteries and wonders of the sea would forever be cherished.

And so, the story of Arielia, the intrepid Sea Angel, continues to inspire new generations to dive into the depths, to embrace the unknown, and to preserve the delicate balance of the ocean's enchanting realm.

* Sea butterflies, 2021, D.G.A, (Digitally drawn, "Coral painter") Tania Winther

Sea Butterflies- Our Guardian Angels.

In the depths of the boundless sea,
Where waves caress with gentle glee,
There dwell ethereal creatures, rare,
Sea Angels, in their realm so fair.

Their bodies delicate, transparent and light,
Glowing softly with a celestial might,
Graceful wings adorned, so fine,
Like heavenly beings, divine.

Beneath the moon's shimmering veil,
They dance with elegance, without fail,
Gliding through the currents with grace,
Leaving trails of wonder in their trace.

Their iridescent beauty casts a spell,
Enchanting all who dare to dwell,
In the realm where dreams come alive,
Where Sea Angels effortlessly thrive.

With every movement, they paint the deep,
Colors of wonder, secrets to keep,
Their wings, a symphony of light,
Guiding lost souls through thc night.

They drift amidst the coral reefs,
Amidst vibrant life, their presence brief,
Their gentle touch, a whispered song,
A reminder that we too belong.

Guardians of the ocean's heart,
They witness its wonders, every part,

From sunlit shallows to depths unknown,
Sea Angels, in their watery throne.
But heed their presence, fragile and pure,
For their world we must help secure,
With every action, let us strive,
To keep their realm alive.

In awe, we gaze upon their flight,
Bathed in moonbeams, a wondrous sight,
Sea Angels, guardians of the sea,
Forever they shall inspire you and me.

Sirens of the Sea

Beneath the waves, where mysteries lie,
In realms of blue, 'neath the sunlit sky,
There dwell enchanting creatures of lore,
Mermaids, whose songs echo forevermore.

Half-human, half-fish, a wondrous sight,
They captivate with their ethereal light,
With flowing locks of seaweed hair,
And shimmering tails, beyond compare.

In ocean depths, where coral blooms,
Their voices soar, dispelling gloom,
Their melodic songs, like ocean breeze,
Carry tales of love and ancient seas.

With eyes as deep as the endless sea,
They hold secrets of eternity,
Their laughter, like pearls, gleaming bright,
Filling the depths with pure delight.

Graceful beings, dancing with the tides,
In harmonious rhythm, their spirits glide,
Through ocean currents, swift and free,
Embodying grace and tranquility.

Legends speak of their fateful charm,
Luring sailors with a siren's harm,
But beneath the surface, lies their truth,
A connection to the sea, their eternal youth.

Protectors of marine realms they be,
Guardians of life beneath the sea,

Their hearts attuned to nature's call,
Preserving the beauty, one and all.

With every shimmering tail's caress,
They weave tales of love and tenderness,
Their presence a blessing, a gentle guide,
Through oceans vast, where wonders hide.

So, dream of mermaids in moonlit nights,
Their splendor shining, their spirits alight,
For in their realm, where fantasy gleams,
Mermaids dwell, forever in dreams.

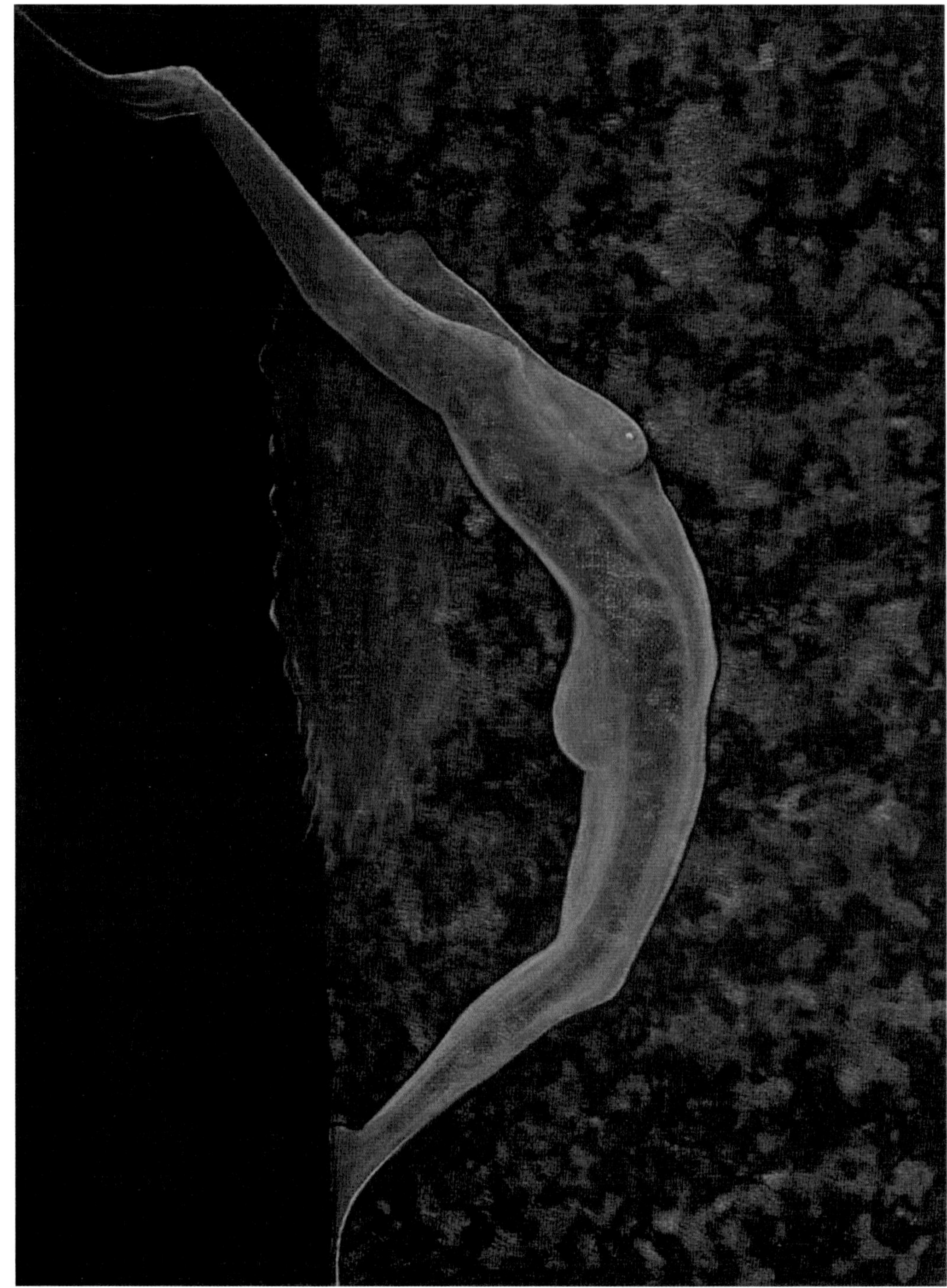

* Translucent, 2021, acrylic painting on canvas, 40x30 cm, Liv Fjellsol.
(Photo: Hege Finsrud)

For the mermaids' song, we'll sing in harmony

In oceans deep, where sadness weeps,
A haunting tale, our heartache keeps,
For mermaids fair, with hearts so pure,
Their song silenced, lost allure.

Once they swam with grace untold,
Amongst the treasures, pearls and gold,
Their laughter echoed through the tide,
A symphony of joy, unbridled pride.

But darkness loomed with human hands,
Pollution spreading across the sands,
The seas, once pristine, now tainted blue,
And mermaids suffered, their lives askew.

With tears of sorrow, their voices waned,
Their vibrant songs became restrained,
As poison seeped into their home,
Silent laments, no longer to roam.

The shimmering tails that once glowed,
Now faded, lifeless, as stories forebode,
Their enchanting beauty, a memory lost,
As human actions came at a cost.

Plastic islands marred the ocean's face,
Tangled nets entwined, a deadly embrace,
Chemical spills, a toxic plight,
Engulfed the mermaids, their sacred right.

Oh, how we weep for what we've done,
Unknowingly, our greed had won,
Our negligence, a heavy toll,
As mermaids slipped beyond our control.

But in this darkness, hope still gleams,
A chance to heal, to mend the seams,
Let's rise as one, with renewed devotion,
To save the seas, with fierce emotion.

For mermaids fading, we must unite,
To restore their realm, bring back the light,
Cleanse the waters, embrace the quest,
Ensure their beauty is forever blessed.

In the depths of regret, we seek redemption,
To undo the harm, reverse the devastation,
To turn the tide, and heal the wounds we've caused,
For the mermaids' sake, their future must be paused.

We gather our strength, our determination strong,
To right the wrongs, where we have gone wrong,
Through awareness and action, we'll make amends,
To ensure the mermaids' story never truly ends.

We rally together, as a force to be reckoned,
Working tirelessly, our efforts interconnected,
Cleaning the oceans, removing the debris,
So that mermaids may once again swim free.

We educate, spreading knowledge and care,
Teaching future generations to be aware,
Of the fragile balance that sustains marine life,
To prevent the mermaids' tragic strife.

Through sustainable practices, we find a way,
To halt the pollution, to save the day,
Investing in technology, innovation in our reach,
To restore the oceans, to save what we beseech.

In this battle against time, we must not falter,
For the mermaids' fate, we are their alter,
With determination in our hearts, we won't rest,
Until the mermaids thrive, once again blessed.

So let us join hands, united in this quest,
To give the mermaids the future they detest,
For in their existence, our world finds wonder,
Let's safeguard their home, with reverence, we ponder.

Together we stand, guardians of the sea,
Preserving the mermaids' legacy,
A testament to the power of our collective might,
To bring back their splendor, to make things right.

For the mermaids' song, we'll sing in harmony,
A symphony of hope, of love, and empathy,
And as the oceans heal, their presence will shine,
Mermaids resilient, a symbol so divine.

In our hands lies their final plea,
To mend the damage, set them free,
Let's rewrite the tale, a different rhyme,
Where mermaids flourish, for all of time.

So, let us strive, with hearts aflame,
To protect their home, their rightful claim,
For in their existence, we find our own,
Let mermaids thrive, forever known.

* Hope, 2023, watercolor & acrylic on paper, 42x60 cm, Tania Winther

Healing Earth

In this world, so vast and wide,
With oceans deep and mountains high,
There's so much beauty to behold,
And so much wonder to unfold.

From the deserts to the seas,
There's so much here to please,
With creatures great and small,
And wonders that enthrall us all.

The sun sets in a fiery blaze,
As night descends with starry gaze,
And in the morning, a new day dawns,
With light that spreads like golden fawns.

Yet, amidst all this beauty and grace,
There's pain and suffering we must face,
From wars that tear us apart,
To hunger that grips our heart.

But hope still shines like a beacon bright,
Guiding us through the darkest night,
And with love and kindness in our hearts,
We can make a world where peace imparts.

So let us work to heal this earth,
To give to it all we're worth,
And may the world, with each passing day,
Grow brighter in every single way.

* Mermaids, 2021, Mixed Media, spray paint & Acrylics on canvas, 50 x 70 cm, Tania Winther

RIDDLE

In ocean depths where currents play,
A gentle voyager lost its way.
Once sleek and free, now trapped in strife,
A tragic tale of marine life.

Its shell, a shield, now binds it tight,
A twisted maze of man-made plight.
Plastic threads weave a deadly crown,
In waters deep, where it's weighed down.

Slowly it swims, a ghostly glide,
In waters where pollutants hide.
A plea for help from nature's plea,
Can you solve this riddle and set it free?

What am I?

Answer: A turtle.

THE END.

As I have reached the end of "Oceans of hope", I am filled with a multitude of emotions. The journey of creating this book has been a learning curve to say the least. Meeting individuals and protectors of the sea combating the pollution and working hard and diligently daily, only to not be fully heard nor understood for what they are contributing with to humanity. It baffles me that we humans are not more conscious about our use of plastic. A product that did not exist over 60 years ago. Now a massive threat to our existence. Ignorance creates bad decisions and poor actions, which again creates terrible consequences.
I have delved deep into the depths of marine littering and ocean pollution, confronting the harsh realities that threaten our oceans.
This book was born out of a collective desire for change, a yearning to raise awareness and ignite a sense of responsibility within us all. What initially started out with creating art exhibitions, with art made out of recycled materials, turned into a book project. By collecting all the poetry I have written over the years into a book, which hopefully will make use as a plea for awareness. I have shed light on the devastating impact of human activities on our marine ecosystems. I have witnessed the cries of marine life silenced by plastic and the silent destruction caused by pollution.
But I have also found solace in the stories of hope that emerged, the tales of individuals and communities who refused to be silent, who took action, and who became the guardians of our seas. I have seen the seeds of change sown and witnessed the power of collective effort in restoring the balance we have disturbed.
As I have come to the end, I hope I have stirred some emotions within you all. We must tread lightly upon the shores and navigate our lives with a renewed sense of reverence for the oceans that sustain us. Let us remember that every choice we make, no matter how small, has the power to create ripples of change.

"Oceans of hope" is not merely a book of poetry; it is a call to action, an invitation to embark on a lifelong commitment to protect and preserve our oceans. It is a reminder that we are custodians of this planet, entrusted with the duty to leave a legacy of beauty and abundance for future generations.
May the words written here continue to echo in your minds and stir your souls. May they inspire you to seek sustainable solutions, advocate for change, and promote a greater harmony between humanity and the oceans that cradle us. The journey doesn't end here; it begins anew, with each step we all take towards a brighter and cleaner future.
Together, let us be the change we wish to see in the world, and create a story of hope, resilience, and reverence for our oceans. For as long as there are activists, poets, politicians and volunteers who speak for the seas, and readers who listen with open hearts, there will always be a chance to heal, to restore, and to ensure that the beauty of our oceans endures for all time.

With my deepest thanks,

Tania Winther

Contributors- A Big Thank You!

From the bottom of my heart, thank you for lending your creative spirit to this endeavor. Your illustrations will continue to ignite the imagination and leave an indelible mark on the hearts of those who experience this book.

Knut Løvås

Løvås is a Norwegian illustrator and artist. He has been a permanent illustrator since 2005 for the Norwegian newspaper "Klassekampen", and is today considered to be one of the country's foremost newspaper illustrators. Løvås has several times been among the finalists in The Newspaper Drawing of the Year Awards, which is awarded each year by the Norwegian Editors Association, the Norwegian Journalists Association and the National Association of Media Companies.

In addition to illustrating current news stories and topics in the daily press, Løvås has also lent the digital brush to other projects. Designing several book covers, both nationally and internationally. With his contribution to this book he has again managed to cleverly illustrate the magnitude of the topic.

https://www.galleri7.com/team-4

Mariel Mikalsen

Mikalsen is a Norwegian artist, writer and art historian major.

Mikalsen has a vivid interest in the sea and nature. She is keen to feed her interests into her art style, which are often beautiful alluring abstract art on canvas. In this book we can see one of her ocean paintings, "Coral Society". Her paintings are made with plastic waste washed up on the shores, which she has inserted into the canvases. They make us yearn to keep the oceans clean and beautiful.

https://www.galleri7.com/team-4

Liv Fjellsol

Fjellsol is a multidisciplinary visual artist and theoretician, who uses art to express her views on contemporary society. Some of her artworks and articles are executed as arts-based research with careful practical and theoretical preparations. The work of art itself developed as a practical visualization of research theories and methods, while also functioning outside of academia as an independent final result or conclusion to be experienced in art exhibitions. Thank you for your evocative and insightful views on this topic through your beautiful and mirthful visual artworks.

www.fjellsol.no

Linda Kristiansen

Kristiansen works conceptually with visual expression, creative stories and themes through the camera lens, combined with digital techniques. Elements and textures are put together to create new expressions and new stories. Some of her works shown in this book is a part of a series Kristiansen has created, depicting a surreal dystopian plastic world. Thank you for your beautiful and yet disturbing contributions of how the world could be if we do not take action.

https://www.lindakristiansen.no/

ABOUT THE AUTHOR

Tania Winther is a multidisciplinary artist, designer, biophiliac and poet hailing from Norway. She has been greatly influenced by her wide and diverse background in both the sciences and the arts, and this comes to surface in her creative expression. Through the interplay of words and visual art, I try to capture a broad spectrum of emotions, inviting readers and viewers to experience my creations on their own terms. Marine littering and ocean pollution is a topic close to my heart. With "Oceans of hope", I embark on a poetic journey that delves into the pressing issue of marine littering and ocean pollution. Through a collection of thought-provoking poems, short stories and haiku, this book aims to raise awareness, inspire action, and shed light on the profound impact of human activities on our oceans. Join me as I explore the depths of this environmental crisis and contemplate the urgent need for change.

"Oceans of hope", endeavors to ignite a sense of responsibility, empathy, and reverence for our oceans. Through a harmonious blend of poetry, prose and evocative illustrations, this book strives to encourage individuals, communities, and policymakers to address the critical issue of marine littering and ocean pollution. Together, let us embark on a transformative journey and safeguard the treasures of the sea for generations to come.

'Art can inspire poetry, and poetry can inspire art'.

If this book has peaked your interest in learning more, please see the list I have compiled for you for further reading on the topic. A list of of super heroes, organizations and companies working hard to combat and achieve solutions:

1.The Ocean Cleanup - A non-profit foundation, founded by Boyan Slat in 2013.
The Ocean Cleanup's team consists of 120 engineers, researchers, scientists, computational modelers, and supporting roles, working daily to rid the world's oceans of plastic.
https://theoceancleanup.com/oceans/

2.Marcus Eriksen- Marine scientist and co-founder of the 5 Gyres Institute studying plastic pollution in the world's oceans.
Co-founder of Leap Lab, a center for art, science and self-reliance.
https://www.marcuseriksen.com/

3. 5 Gyres Institute
Marcus Eriksen and Anna Cummins founded the 5 Gyres Institute to investigate key unanswered questions about plastic pollution: *How much plastic is floating in the world's oceans? Where is it accumulating? Is it causing harm to people and the planet? And most importantly,* ***what can we do about it?*** They have explored 50,000 nautical miles in search of plastic on 19 research expeditions, publishing groundbreaking research, building a global network of ambassadors, and inspiring change along the way.
https://www.5gyres.org/

4.Leap Lab
https://www.leaplab.org/our-philosophy

5.Ocean works
In 2016 our founder Rob Ianelli created Norton Point, a mission-oriented brand which debuted the use of ocean plastics in eyewear. In creating Norton Point, Rob witnessed first-hand the challenges of navigating the fragmented, disorganized ocean plastic sector. It was clear that someone needed to roll up their sleeves and do something to close the gap on supply and meet consumer demand at scale. In 2018, Oceanworks was born.
https://oceanworks.co/

6.Sea life trust
https://www.sealifetrust.org/en/how-to-help/reduce-plastic-litter/

7.Plastic pollution coalition
Plastic Pollution Coalition is a non-proft commuications and advocacy organization that collaborated with an expansive global alliance of organizations, businesses, and individuals to create a more just, equitable, regenerative world free of plastic pollution and its toxic impacts.
https://www.plasticpollutioncoalition.org/about

8. Greenpeace
Greenpeace is a global organization working to stop environmental crimes, using non-violent creative action. The main goals of the group are to protect biodiversity in all its forms, prevent pollution and abuse of the earth's ocean, land, air, and fresh water, end all nuclear threats, promote peace, global disarmament, and non-violence The organization works towards several issues pertaining to the marine environment in particular. With its vast networks across the world, Greenpeace argues big corporations to reduce their plastic footprint to end the flow of plastic into our oceans. In addition, the organization is also engaged in addressing unsustainable industrial fishing practices, climate change, and ocean acidification.

9.World Wildlife Fund
The World Wildlife Fund is another one of the world's leading conservation organizations. It works in 100 countries and is supported by more than one million members in the United States and close to five million globally. WWF's unique way of working combines global reach with a foundation in science, involves action at every level from local to global, and ensures the delivery of innovative solutions that meet the needs of both people and nature. Among the WWF's top priorities in the area of marine conservation are working with fishers, fishing companies and scientists around the globe to understand and meet sustainability standards; working with organizations around the world toward the goal of expanding the extent of mangrove cover around the world 20% by the year 2030; and safeguarding the Arctic through advancing climate-smart, sustainable development, and securing permanent protection for ecologically critical areas.

10.The Nature Conservancy
The Nature Conservancy is one of the oldest and most respected conservation organizations in the world. Established in 1951, the organization has over 1 million members and works to protect ecologically important lands and waters at the largest scale. As for marine conservation, in particular, the Nature Conservancy operates more than 100 of such projects globally. Some of them include work to create sustainable fisheries, while protecting and restoring fish habitat; mapping ocean wealth and incorporating the gathered information into decision-making; improving the health of coral reefs; protecting the coastlines, etc.

11.The Coral Reef Alliance
The Coral Reef Alliance works with communities around the world, helping to solve coral reef conservation challenges. Through collaboration with fishermen, government leaders, divers, and scientists the organization leads holistic conservation programs that improve coral reef health and resilience and are replicated across the globe. The majority of the work is done in four critically important reef regions of the world - Fiji, Hawaii, Indonesia, and the Mesoamerican Region. Globally, CORAL is launching a new era of reef conservation that facilitates coral adaptation to a changing climate and expands the scientific understanding of coral conservation. The Alliance's signature initiatives include: Healthy Fisheries for Reefs, Clean Water for Reefs, Intact Reef Ecosystems, and Science of Adaptation.
12.Sea Shepherd Conservation Society
Although somewhat controversial, this organization definitely deserves attention. Founded by Paul Watson, a former member of Greenpeace, in 1977, under the name Earth Force Society, the organization is now best known for obstructing Japanese whaling activities in the Southern Ocean. Sea Shepherd aims to end the destruction of habitat and slaughter of wildlife in the world's oceans in order to conserve and

protect ecosystems and species. They use innovative direct-action non-lethal tactics including scuttling and disabling whaling vessels, intervening in seal hunts and throwing bottles of foul-smelling butyric acid onto whaling vessels at sea, among others.

13.Marine Megafauna Foundation
As the name suggests, the MMF focuses specifically on research and conservation for threatened marine-megafauna species, such as sharks, rays, marine mammals and turtles. Founded in 2003, the organization initially was working with the large population of marine megafauna found along the Mozambican coastline. In recent years, however, MMF researchers have expanded their efforts worldwide. The MMF's current research focuses on species-level population ecology and conservation biology. The organization also works to improve the management of existing marine protected areas (MPAs) and develop effective, long-term conservation strategies to protect and restore key habitats. On a regional level, it is a trusted conservation leader, empowering local communities to manage marine resources sustainably.

14. Monterey bay Aquarium
The nonprofit Monterey Bay Aquarium is a showcase for the habitats and sea life of one of the world's richest marine regions. In addition to that, the organization coordinates marine conservation and research programs. The Aquarium is helping to save species like sea otters and white sharks, and giving a voice to urgent ocean issues at the local, state, national and international levels. The Aquarium's Conservation and Science programs are tackling some of the most critical issues affecting ocean health. The Aquarium conducts research in the fields of population biology and ecology of sharks, bluefin tuna and sea otters. Finally, through their Seafood Watch program, the organization helps consumers and businesses choose seafood that's fished or farmed in ways that support a healthy ocean.

15.Project AWARE foundation
Project AWARE Foundation is an organization working specifically with scuba divers across the globe to protect underwater environments. Focused on the critical issues of Shark Conservation and Marine Debris, Project AWARE empowers thousands to work together for a clean, healthy and abundant ocean planet. If you want to take part in one of the organization's campaigns, you can explore the current Action Map to find the upcoming events or even create your own event. You can also adopt a dive site to engage in ongoing, local protection and monitoring of a particular area, start a fundraiser with Project Aware or donate to the organization.

16.Oceana
Oceana is the largest organization in the world solely devoted to marine conservation. It was established in 2001 by The Pew Charitable Trusts, the Oak Foundation, Marisla Foundation, and Rockefeller Brothers Fund. Since its founding, Oceana has achieved hundreds of concrete policy victories for marine life and habitats. As part of its campaigns, Oceana is involved in efforts to end major sources of ocean pollution such as oil, mercury, aquaculture and shipping emissions. In addition to that, the organization also campaigns for the protection of vulnerable places in the oceans, including the Arctic, the Aleutian Islands, the Mediterranean and Chile's Juan Fernandez Islands, among others.

17.The Ocean Conservancy
Ocean Conservancy is another leading advocacy group working for the protection of special marine habitats, the restoration of sustainable fisheries, and for reducing the human impact on ocean ecosystems. Founded in 1972, the organization was initially known as the Delta Conservancy and later the Center for Environmental Education and the Center for Marine Conservation before receiving its current name. In order to save our oceans, the group focuses on educating the public and advocating for policy changes for maintaining vibrant ocean wildlife. One of Ocean Conservancy's best-known efforts is the International Coastal Cleanup program. The annual cleanups bring millions of volunteers all over the world together to collect and document the trash littering their coastline.

18.Surfrider organisation
https://www.surfrider.org/

19.Ocean Blue Project
https://oceanblueproject.org/

20.Marine Bio
https://www.marinebio.org/conservation/marine-conservation-biology/organizations/

21.Plastic Oceans
https://plasticoceans.org/

22.Innovations oceans sans plastique- NGOs and organizations around the world.
https://innovations-oceans-sans-plastique.com/en/ngo-from-a-z/

23.Plastic free oceans
https://plasticfreeoceans.org/

24.Zoos Victoria - Fighting Extinction
https://www.zoo.org.au/

25.Take 3 for the sea.
https://www.take3.org/

26.The Story of Stuff project
https://www.storyofstuff.org/

27.I million women
https://www.1millionwomen.com.au/

28.Plastic change- Denmark
https://plasticchange.dk/

29.Exxpedition
https://exxpedition.com/

30.Lonely Whale
https://www.lonelywhale.org/

31.Plastic Free July
https://www.plasticfreejuly.org/

32.Open Oceans Global
https://www.openoceans.org/

33.Beyond Plastics
https://www.beyondplastics.org/

34. GALLERY 7/URBAN ART - NORWAY
Galleri 7 in Norway has made an art project with several artists and designers making art from recycled plastic washed up from the shores. It is an interdisciplinary art exhibition making us question the marine pollution and plastic waste problems increasing today. An ever changing and movable art exhibition, popping up in several places with the intention to spread awareness.
"Exploring the Ocean-Aftermath of Humanity".
https://www.galleri7.com/projects-6

Made in United States
Orlando, FL
15 December 2023